froglets
Learners

Sea Life

by Annabelle Lynch

First published in 2014 by
Franklin Watts
338 Euston Road
London NW1 3BH

Franklin Watts Australia
Level 17/207 Kent Street
Sydney NSW 2000

Copyright © Franklin Watts 2014

Picture credits:
Allnaturalbeth/Dreamstime: 21. Sergio Bertino/
Dreamstime: 6. Neil Bradfield/Dreamstime: 7. Rich
Carey/Shutterstock: 11. Deborah Coles/Dreamstime:
20. Cosmopol/Dreamstime: 15. gilmar/Shutterstock:
5. pierre j/Shutterstock: 16. Kelpfish/Dreamstime: 12.
Photo Researchers/FLPA: 19. Piboon Srimak/
Dreamstime: 8.

Every attempt has been made to clear copyright.
Should there be any inadvertent omission please
apply to the publisher for rectification.

Contents

The words in **bold** can be found in the glossary.

On the shore

Hermit crabs live on the **shore**. When they are **attacked**, they hide away in their shell!

Hermit crabs live in the empty shells of other sea creatures.

Rockpools

Colourful sea anemones live in rockpools. They look like flowers but can give you a nasty sting!

Coral reef

Coral reefs are made up of millions of tiny animals. They join together to form a reef. Coral is different colours. It can be hard or soft, round or pointed, spiky or smooth.

Coral reefs grow slowly over time.

Reef life

Lots of sea creatures live on a coral reef, including octopuses. They have eight legs, but no **bones**, so they can squeeze into small gaps on the reef.

If an octopus is attacked, it can squirt out black ink!

Sharks

Sharks live in the open ocean. They are great **hunters** and can swim very fast to chase their **prey** of fish and other sea creatures.

Sharks may look scary, but most won't harm you.

Whales

Whales are the biggest animals that live in the sea. They swim across whole oceans to feed and to have their babies.

Whales live in the sea, but they are **mammals**, not fish.

Dolphins

Dolphins are friendly and playful. They can leap right out of the water and they love to follow boats.

Dolphins swim in groups called pods.

Deep sea fish

The black seadevil lives
in the deep, dark sea.
It has a light above its
mouth. Little fish come
to look at the light.
Then the seadevil
eats them up!

Lots of animals that live in the deep sea make their own light.

Weird and wonderful

Pufferfish are some of the strangest sea creatures. When they are attacked they swallow water to blow up into a big, spiky ball!

Pufferfish can be **poisonous** to other fish and to people.

21

Glossary

attack – to try to hurt something

bones – the hard parts inside our body. Together they make up our skeleton

hunter – a creature that eats other creatures

mammal – animals with hair that give birth to babies. They feed their babies with milk

poisonous – containing poison. Poison can harm or even kill you

prey – a creature that is eaten by another creature

shore – a place where the sea meets the land

Websites:

http://www.nhm.ac.uk/kids-only/life/life-sea/
http://ocean.nationalgeographic.com/ocean/ocean-life/

Quiz

1. What do hermit crabs live in?

2. Where are rockpools found?

3. How many legs does an octopus have?

4. What do sharks eat?

5. What are the biggest animals that live in the sea?

6. What do pufferfish do when they are attacked?

The answers are on page 24

Answers

1. Shells
2. On rocky shores
3. Eight
4. Fish and other sea creatures
5. Whales
6. Swallow water to blow up into a spiky ball

Index